AF480643

Playing with Phosphenes

Sabine Ruh House

Cover Letter

'He [Camillo] pretends that all things that the human mind can conceive and which we cannot see with the corporeal eye, after being collected together by diligent meditation, may be expressed by certain corporeal signs in such a way that the beholder may at once perceive with his eyes everything that is otherwise hidden in the depth of the human mind..'- [The Memory Theatre of Giulio Camillo, from the Dime-Store Alchemy: The Art of Joseph Cornell by Charles Simic]

I have been dabbling in poetry since I was a child. Sometimes certain words and phrases come together to give a sensation, which I can only call synesthesia. I keep searching for that feeling. Some others might call it joy.

I share with Sally Mann what she terms a Magpie's aesthetic: a spontaneous and constructive act of picking from the landscape of conception anything I find interesting. That which dazzles my corporeal eye, I put together into corporeal signs. My creations just happen to have a verbal expression. And sometimes with no overarching references; like her, I too write just for fun, so to speak. Barbara Guest's words from "Wounded Joy", beautifully capture my own sense of play while writing, she says 'I know that I have accidentally typed a wrong word and thought, "well that's a better word, anyway."

I think William Kentridge puts it well when he says that optimistic and pessimistic results are obtained together all the time, and the outcome is never the rapture of rationality. He propounds that the self is contradictory, and chaos is in fact the norm. And this entire collection, is nothing if not chaotic. As in Gogol's "The Nose", the absurd may be impossible, but it is also true that the impossible is what happens all the time.

You might think my poetry runs everywhere and nowhere all at once, but it is really the sense of play I would like to leave you with.

It takes a village, and I've had the honor and privilege of being surrounded by the best.

-My Mom, who had me reciting poetry at a very young age and instilled in me a love of rhymes. She made up bedtime stories, which cultivated a love of improvisation. Maybe that is why, to date, not following the recipe doesn't faze me. It keeps me motivated. Growing up, a good story was the greatest escape I could hope to find.

-My Dad and his love of books. He also has a knack for storytelling, which he passed on to me. Try listening to one of his stories, without cracking a smile, I dare you.

-Every single one of my literature and poetry teachers through the years. I remain in awe of what you accomplish in the length of a semester

-Friends who urged me to write and applauded and cheered my fledgling attempts as only friends can do.

-My editors who spent hours refining the poems and giving them structure. Their kind words helped me believe these poems were worth publishing. We all need hype buddies, and they were mine.

Last but certainly not in the least, my incredible partner, who gave me space, time and infinite resources to do what I do.

With my best,

CONTENTS

1. WHIM-SIMICAL

Stage set
Doused in blue.
Theatrics even before
The act started,
Lights out, the theatre darkens,
A hopeful hush, undeniable magic,
Hope is magic
And maybe magic is hope.

A whirl, a twirl,
A graceful girl
Pirouetting with the crowd's expectation,
Preening for posterity,
Sinewy blue limb outstretched,
Defying gravity,
Her defiant tutu
Lifting beyond the imagination,
Far beyond dreams
And real life,
Enacting the white swan,
Or was it grey?

Beauty is the act
Of metamorphosing
So seamlessly
That the viewer forgets
The fragments
For the dazzling,

Unutterable whole,
So beautiful is the act,
Your heart breaks
To realize it's not real.

Every part, separated
From the act,
Has and always had a life
Of its own.

- Based on artwork in *Dime-store Alchemy* by Charles Simic

2. PFANNTASTIC PANNENKOEK HAUS

Out of nowhere,
In he walked.
Military green jacket,
Eyebrows raised
As if surprised
To walk out of the imperfect poetry
I had been writing since I was ten.

Color like I had never seen before,
Like the visible spectrum, burst open -
'*You can never go back,*'he said.

From the first time,
Dark hair, green eyes for life,
Green, the shade of chrysoprase,
Aquamarine,
Gifts to show he cared.

A perfect branch of pale pink
Cherry blossoms, their petals intact,
That replaced
A single red rose
That never stopped blooming,
Still sitting in a clear vase
On the living room table,
By the ivory charmeuse curtains,
I had him put up
While we both waited for me

To open my eyes.

Heartbreak in champagne topaz eyes -
That and broken familial ties,
Chalcedony
Could rhyme with treachery,
Grief rises in my throat,
Making it hard to breathe.

Every-day mist with bread,
Water and hyacinths,
Maddeningly reminiscent
Of Vancouver streets -
Of promise, of change
In Albertan blue skies,
When we chased pots of gold
At the end of the rainbow.

Promise and change, I left behind
For everyday mist
In the smokey grey
Quartz of my eyes.

Now he is teaching me
How to drive again.
His rough hands on mine
As the gear shifts,
Later, my friend alludes to
Me as 'morning',
And to him as 'night',
As if morning and night

Have not followed each other
Since time immemorial.

Now, there is a visible tremor
In his right hand and I ask,
'What gives?'
As I reach out to steady him,
He does not withdraw,
But there's a quiet rebuff
To not tend to the garden
I would then abandon,
Bittersweet, in a prison
Of my own making.

Wistfully I trace
The physical outline of a key,
Chalcedony
Could rhyme with treachery.

Knowing champagne topaz eyes
Offering bread, water and hyacinths,
M in all her wisdom cites
Apologues of boiling a frog,
'He will wear you down,' she says,
Referring to sly topaz eyes.

Treachery is not unique to me.
While I busy myself in books and papers,
Hiding the everyday mist,
Finding medical solutions for all and sundry,
I push down the grief rising

Till I can't breathe,
I cannot breathe.

Now he jams his arm
Next to mine,
And my heart lurches
With the trapeze artist
At Cirque du Soleil
We paid to see,
Instead, he is looking sideways,
Amused at the audible
March-past in my throat.

Now its lilac season,
And we are amidst the pine,
He is talking about fly fishing,
"Always with the fishing," I think.
Eyes closed, by the Bow River,
Green the shade of chrysoprase,
Aquamarine,
And he can feel a cool shiver
Before it rises down my spine.
'*Never again,*' he says,
As we both think
Of champagne topaz eyes,
And I leave,
Leaving him a bottle
Of sandalwood,
Mirroring the haze
In the smokey grey
Quartz of my eyes.

Every year I wait for lilac season,
When purple adorns my street,
Across from my brownstone,
My French windows frame
Wild lilac shrubbery
That came calling
As soon as I moved here.
As if the lilac didn't trust
The memories
That sprang up
Every so often,
To bring me back
Across the border.

My tortoise shell glasses intellectualize,
Even as the ivory charmeuse curtains rip
The second I land in Chicago
And miss the smell of pine.

Staring desolately out of the car,
Drawn by familial strings
Downtown to my condo,
Overlooking Lake Michigan,
Green the shade of chrysoprase,
Aquamarine,
Tidal reminder
Of the seven cups of coffee
And content I left behind
At the Dutch pancake house
Back in Calgary.

3. Pin the Donkey

It's not
Birds singing
Or ethereal light
It's everyday coffee
And contentment
On the porch
Of our life
Side by side
Our rough
And tumble home
Last white notes
On the entrails of a sigh
When I exhale smoke
I only breathe-in to deny
You only nod
When you complete
'Where have you been'-
with
'All my life'

4. Vocation

Suddenly I met
You, your love
Was a heady mix,
You didn't
Keep me from joy
Like he did,
I learnt from him
To keep some
Of me for myself
And not give away
Everything to
My object of affection.

I try but it's hard,
We are happy,
Maybe we don't
Have enough
But we make
Each other laugh
And you are
Imperfectly mine,
And it's real
And maybe I love
Your friends
And family
Or maybe I don't
But you are not afraid
To hold my hand

When we see them,
Barely as we stand
Guard over
Each other's solitudes.

Ideas and new places
Our closest friends
As we keep each other
Company.

5. THE THIEF

Surf rolls down the
Brow of the beach
Sand grains lost
In the flux
Green onyxes mined
On the ocean floor
Raise their incendiary
Faces to the light
Envy rises, rolled up at a glance,
Light through a different prism,
Words stringed like pearls,
Around another fair neck.
The wind howls as the waves crest

Yet the sound is singular.
I recognize the thief of joy
And look away
Tuning out the wind howling
Against my window
Focusing instead,
On the climbing tidewater
Blues of the floral white cotton
Against my morning
Soft breaths in as the gentle
Machinations of this
lakeview morn take over
Salving my dithering rumination

6. NEITHER STARS NOR WILDFLOWERS

It's nearly 3 am
And I am sitting here,
Spinning wheels,
Weaving tales of the choicest words
Like I'm going to live forever,
Like the years will wait for me,
Like you will,
Just because
You know I have trouble
Telling you what's on my mind.

As if my trauma
Is any of your business,
Like you'll kiss my onyx hair
While I'm hard at work,
Bring me rhubarb
With salt
For my wounds,
On all my late nights
And lack of words.

As if your green eyes haven't
Already forgotten
The smokey grey quart
Of my hooded gaze.

Like you'll always
Stand a little too close,

Perhaps breathing in
Coconut cream whiffs
Of my freshly conditioned hair,
Asking me to wear something sexy
To your shindig
In the garage you rent,
Already somehow knowing
My tiny frame
Beneath my baggy clothes,
(Your disdain apparent
For the 'baggy' in my 'clothes').

Like you'll always
Come pick me up from work
At rush hour,
When I twist my ankle
And need a friend,
Against your better judgement
And your friend's advice.
As if you will always
Suddenly appear
When I'm thinking about you,
Brooding at the house,
Or standing in line
At the fair,
Seeking me,
As my mind sought you.

As if you, too, were waiting,
Hoping we may, somehow,
Inexplicably, meet again.

But now you've gently let go
Of my pink bathrobe
I deliberately left,
With the memory
Of my bare pink toes -
You held onto for six years.

7. Forget-me-nots

It should be easy
To forget
Maybe if our conversations
Hadn't rocked my boat,
Shocking me out of the house,
Stacked with everything
I had already known,
Or if the sound of
Your lilting French outside my room
On the stairs,
With someone in stilettos,
Didn't get a sympathetic
Visceral response.

Or if you hadn't turned around
On the green porch
Outside our house,
To stare at me in disbelief
Through the charmeuse curtains
I had you put up.
Back on the couch,
After my trip home,
Dark glasses shielding me
From the memory
Of your hurt, mossy green eyes.
Feeling inexplicably
Soiled by your attention.

Your messages
Had gone unanswered,
Where you recognized
My sunshine state of mind,
You were the last man
To observe,
As if already jaded
By my choices,
When you noted
Those past six months
Would be the most fun
I'd ever have
Till years later,
Out with a group of people
We both knew,
A pair of champagne topaz eyes
Sitting diagonally,
Watching me, remarked
I sounded like sunshine
On a cold day
When Moscato was involved.

8. TRUNNION BASCULE BRIDGE

You are not yet comfortable
Around my edges
Unsure of the broken bits,
The jagged forms,
Come as surprises.
And I flinch,
As you make your way.
I show you how to tread,
Feather your steps,
Muffle with moss,
Brown the green,
I let you softly dust-
-off the stories,
You see traced in stone.
Or spots your curious
Fingers need to explore.
I let you in,
Gossamer-ed in hope

9. It's my party and I'll cry if I want to

I have bared
Myself to this friendly sheet,
Gingerly placed memories
In tiny shining bows,
Glittered with dew,
So, I can move on
And create more.

In a stranger's eyes,
Looking through the
French windowpanes
Of my charming brownstone,
It must be sublime -
This well-lit, terrific dark
Of chocolate mousse,
I knew you would get
From my favorite baker
Or the splendid bouquet
Of sunflowers blended
With the bright pink of roses,
Against the pale
Smattering of peonies
You placed on our white counter,
So, I could wake up
To color *tous le jours*.

It is the blue in the
Violet forget-me-nots

That holds my gaze,
Wishing that
Chrysoprase
Of foreign eyes
Was part of the fray.

10. PHOSPHENES

Phosphenes left by
The glare of the sun
Reflected in my rearview
Seen with a stranger
Tachycardiatic when he
Messaged years later
And twenty years fade
Into the background, when
Looking at you,
With your champagne topaz eyes,
Was like gazing at the sun.

Incredulous for someone
Who held security so dear,
To regard in vivid color
Images from
A six-month stint -
Words played, and replayed,
As I weave in and out
Of scenes that brighten
Exponentially with time.

As if it hasn't been seven years -
As if he hadn't told me that
Hard work and a soft bed
Was all we'd need,

As if my friends didn't red flag
My need for stability.
It was as if
Ancestral discontent
Took hold on the sly,
Mystifying my needs,
I heard my mother's voice
As I stood helpless
In its wake
In trying not to make
The mistakes they made,
I seemed to have made
Every. Last. One.

Hope is that creeper;
Like English Ivy, variegated,
Its roots slithering and sliding
Through this mortal coil
To the ventricles of my brain,
Furtively from seeds sown
By phosphenes
In the years past,
Hope wormed its way up
From the chambers
Of my heart.

In devastating
Green flourish now

Propagating itself,
Thriving, if you will,
On any and all
Nourishment
Coming its way;
Inadvertent fuel
From stray phosphenes
Of my own discontent.

11. Round pegs in square holes

Something is missing
And it has been missing
For a while,
Something doesn't feel right
When I listen to you,
Brushing it off
Like its benign,
Like your rugged face
Across me at Carmine's,
Is not in sync
With your words,
I don't see them align
Like round pegs
In square holes.

They are not bitter,
Just different
Like I was tuned in
To another
Conversation
I especially enjoyed
And now the receiver is broken,
It can't detect you
Like you can't
See the mild frown between
The smokey quartz
Of my eyes.

Your words
Are less foreign
Than the ones
I now receive
But the sweetness
Has left the languages
We do speak,
You've had my heart
From day one,
I've put it in everything you
But although I hear
Your words,
There's an indifference
Almost like you are waiting
For bad news.

Maybe your heart
Sank for a reason
The two times
I left your side
And your champagne
Topaz eyes reddened
Preparing for our
Final goodbye.

12. Educated

I'm not privy
To the auspices
Of these ivy
Wrapped halls
Grateful for
Hall passes
I grab a glimpse
of words, in a
Quadrangle
Its road cobbled
With prestige
Rooms curtained
In layered fabric
Held together
By haloed gold
Strings of
Whispered gasps
Gathering
For, at least,
A century

I make the most
Of the twenty
Rickety miles
I walked to
be refused
I absorb
Every crevice

Every nook
Every street lamp
And your
Seasonal blossoms
In late March
Outside the glass dome
Years spent exalting
Your sentinels,
In adoration.
Phosphenes
Now at my
Beck and call
I win
I win
I win

13. SAN FRANCISCO

Your steady is unstudied
It was mapped in your cells
Long before you.
And I've reveled in it
Through the years.
As you decisively
Held on. Calling me
Out of many a muddled spell
Giving me directions
Blue eyes
Like cornflowers melted into crystal
Focused on me occasionally
Hair lighter in the sun
Even as you embody the
gentleness of the moon

14. Voltaire

She took it to heart
When Voltaire said
To cultivate your own garden,
She stops to ask almost offhandedly
Like a sideways glance was enough,
How I'd celebrate
What treatment was offered,
For the pain I'd been in
And my short reply suffices
To take her off course
From my discomfort
When I need a friend,
Almost like my burden
Will always be my own
Like she cannot see through
My easy gaiety,
Even as she bares her soul
Not shying away from the
Gory everyday
Vulgarity.

I do not need to be burdened with
But I am all over it
Despite my day,
So now I take her advice
And cultivate my own,
Keeping my afflictions private,
Ones she was too busy to share

Ploughing through,
Somehow knowing it will be okay
If I can just breathe through
This one last thought
Before I am too spent
To stay upright
And gently let go.

15. The Handmaid's Tale

I am a slice of
An illustrious land,
I am free,
With freedom
To be wild -
Brave, feline
Of the tempestuous kind.

Everywhere I see
There is acceptance,
Back-to-back,
Just a collage of creeds,
With resolute bonds
And determined ties.

Our beliefs
Above absolution,
No creature
Do we exclude -
Just harmless
Harmony,
Absolute.

Genetics help
Tear apart
What may otherwise
Just be blood,
Muscle

And pounding heart.

Anger, envy,
Grief and love,
There is nothing here
That I am above.

- Based on Rene Magritte - *Mesdemoiselles De Lisle Adam*

16. This Old House

This old house:
It creaks too much,
Soft treads are lost
With the mischievous crouch,
I cannot creep up,
I cannot creep down,
My kids cannot
Not make a sound,
Neither hide
Nor seek
Without
Loud creaks
That reveal
The arrival
Of little feet
Trudging up,
Trudging down,
All my neighbors
Agree
A hundred years is too old
For a house to be.

17. Fatherhood

If the whole idea
Behind living a wonderful life
Is to do what gives you joy,
I think I might be satisfied
With putting pen to paper -
I don't need
To create life from scratch -
To feed it, to burp it,
To have it smile back at me,
Eyes crinkling
In the image of the smokey grey quartz
Of my eyes,
Wild onyx curls amok,
I'm not built like him,
He needs
More than images birthed
On this sheet
To feed his joy,
To have it expand
In his thoracic cage
And pump more than it did
Before the birthday.

I can still smile
Like I've smiled
Every day since I was ten
And found,
Almost by accident,

Those rhymes
Fueled by epinephrine,
Imagine my delight
At having birthed
So many kids
I didn't have to burp
Or feed.

18. Under your tutelage

I am only acquainted
With the inflections
Of your tone
Your sun
Hasn't warmed
My doorway
And your shadows
Haven't darkened
My halls
I haven't
Breathed in
The soft wisps
Of your presence
And my cells
Are as yet
Unsullied by anything
less than care
Engorged only
By the fullest
Of your attention
I oft think
Your thoughts reside
In a garden of roses
Of the softest pink
In an everbloom
Swaying in
Soft scents of
Harmony

19. I'LL RESONATE TO THIS

Is it just me
Who imagines
A sleeping form
At His feet, encased
In His Golden Light
When I'm defeated
And distraught
And no words of comfort
Were brought
By the closest of kin?

I don't understand religion
And its need for
A show -
Maybe it brings people together,
Creates a vibe
A frequency,
We can collectively resonate to
Energy to move my atoms
Just as it moves yours

That does sound nice
But in its absence,
For now,
I'll be the sleeping form
At His feet, encased
In His Golden Light
When I'm defeated
And distraught.

20. In my house, it's always Christmas

I'm sitting upside
Down as if
I don't aspire
To an ambitious
To-do list
Of somber questions
Meant to hone
My skills.

Looking at a life sized
Portrait of an arty
Fashionista, I am not
In all her size zero
Glory I so adored
For years, when
The mistletoe I've
Quietly loved,
Hanging nondescript
On the layered trim,
All seasons of the year,
Was always there
By her very side -
To accept me for my
Erring ways.

21. FROM SALLY'S LENS

Foliage frames the vast spans,
Prescient exposure to the flow,
Waiting for some
Incendiary light,
Some gentle fluidity,
A solitary tree, the king
Of all he surveys,
Branches eviscerating the distance
Between earth and sky.

Trying to indenture
Its environ, an ambitious
Melancholic stretch,
Hard to disregard
This zealous demagogue -
In the foreground,
Its ominous shape twisted
In elegant knots,
Already calling to action,
With unscrupulous whispers
Made in the silvery silence,
The still lake, reluctant
To take sides,
Its silvery silence on loan
From the sky,
 A fickle friend;
Its silver seeping
Into callous dark clouds.

At the pastoral vanguard,
A grassy plain, presumably green
Or bronze,
Some sly shrubbery
Quiet yet not quite
Engaging with the still lake.

- Based on Sally Mann Deep South, Untitled (Weyanoke
Estate, Louisiana), 1998

22. Out of Control

I've taken to growing
Basil and mint
In my little kitchen
Off Surf Street
Where I propagate
The living hell out
Of these herbs,
So much so that now
Their unkempt
Branches adorn
Every surface
Of my rough
And tumble
Home,
Which they seemed
To have taken a keen liking
To because why else
Would they grow
With such grave abandon,
As if ours was the
Only home
On Pine Grove
With any nourishment
To offer?

23. For a second, then I split

I took an instant
Liking to watercolor
Pastels, in life
Like shapes meant to
Still life for a small
Second in my day.

As my eyes contour
The forms
They make, minimal
On white backgrounds
With baby blue pixelated
Sketches in designer
Wear, I refuse to
Afford yet wear
In that small blurred
Second in my day.

24. AND SO WE FETE

The crowd pulsed
With a sweet hope,
Some eyes sparkled,
While that one recluse moped.

We were celebrating change
In this carnival called Life.
At the prospect, some rejoiced
And some shivered.

Change, her advent,
Was devastating but real.
She was to walk in with grief
And growth at her heel,
This was, in fact, the turn of the wheel.
I saw some withdraw, defeated,
While some others
Were at an even keel.

She heckled Nature,
Her ever-enduring spouse,
He was known to be bold,
But could be meek of stature.

Her charms disarm
Every peasant in the swarm,
No one could escape her call;
Neither load bearing animal

Nor ostentatiously dressed feature.

She welcomes us all
To the cosmic ball,
We bow gallantly,
It was protocol.

Looking her in the eye,
I did not reel,
Knowing my present
Was for her to steal.

- Based on *The Liver is the Cock's Comb*, Arshile Gorky

25. MORTALITY

I hoard these
Old books
From all over the world,
Of authors my
Father used to read,
Decking all my shelves
With stories
From his and his brother's
Boyhood libraries -
Relics for when
They are gone.

Pages that will still speak,
The spines are getting old,
Feeble like my father's bones.

Every once in a while
The binding falls apart
And my dad brings out his
Portable pharmacy,
There was one book,
14 years in the making,
Based on a dog,
A Tibetan Lhasa apso
My Dad had
Cared for dearly.

When we lost that book,

Mysteriously,
Right on the verge
Of a long journey
Where the little beast
Would have
Kept us company,
My father couldn't find
Anything to mend
The now lifeless bind,
Although he did search
His whole pharmacy.

26. Blue

I've been in your shoes
My little nose against the
Cold glass watching the blue
Cool colors against the November sky
Blushing coral of the fading sun
Some embers of light still alive
With spectacular indifference to your day
dressed to the nines at your funeral service
Blue so bright you can't look away
Why do you get to stay,
While I'm called away.

27.When the Magpie hit the Gallows

In a land where men forsake
True words, who will tell
My story, but birds?

Bruegel's magpies with whiplash
Wits, relate moral tales
In otherwise
Worldly skits.

It's the State
Putting on a show
For piety's sake, crass
Fallacy is at stake;
It's the Puppet-master State.

Though irate, can the people cry
Without their lives going awry?
To the gallows they go,
Along with their wives.

Amidst this anarchy,
These very dire straits,
Life passes you by
At an idyllic rate,
In an idyllic state.

- Based on *The Magpie on the Gallows* by Pieter Bruegel
the Elder

28. Let's Face It

The diamond is for sale
She wills pretty things,
Tokens from her marriage,
Twelve years ago,
When she couldn't stop
Smiling, her eyes alive,
Dancing in flouncy hems,
Silhouette glammed,
Into brick walls and a roof
To keep herself subsisted
Till she gets a job,
A different dance
Her employer
Getting a whiff
Of her desperation
Will undercut
What she could otherwise make,
Unless her mother
Who continues to low ball
What she could do
Finds her in a particularly
Vulnerable state
And thrusts a
Job for undergrads
Without degrees.

Ma meant well
But will get her

Pound of flesh
Anyway,
The vultures have been circling
For a taste
Of the carcass,
Of abused
Meat and bones,
It's a worn out
Boiled frog,
Wasn't much to begin with,
But the predators
Need to eat, too.

29. This is not a Love story

I am too smart for love poems;
All my degrees
Belie my ego,
But my heart is a cliché -
Same old trope…
Strung along by love stories
Of a single red rose
That was in bloom
Until I tossed it out,
Into the blue sky
With broken glass
In a black trash bag.

Not before the glass
Gashed open my palm,
As if warning me
To retrace my path,
While I looked over
At chrysoprase eyes,
Silently protesting
Across the yard
From the kitchen window,
As I stood doing dishes
He didn't want me doing,
Only half glancing
At my heart
Halfway across the yard,
Hidden in the violet twilight.

As if the Owl was not
Athena's totem,
As if I didn't wear her
Like an albatross around my neck,
Thrusting wisdom
And strategy under
My tortoiseshell glasses,
Even when my heart is a cliché,
Same old trope…
Writing love poems,
Sitting at my white kitchen counter
In my charming brownstone,
Hidden in the violet twilight
Even though the bleach I buy
Cannot clean
The crimson rusting stains
Of tissue smeared
Across the counter.

This giant gash opens,
Obscured by the violet twilight.

Only half glancing,
Halfway across the border,
Hidden in the violet twilight.

- Based on Cy Twombly: *"The Fire"*

30. DAWN

Misted spring mornings
Dew on you, on me,
Sprinkled on us sleeping,
Dreaming kindred dreams.

31. Bias

Banality of bias
Placates for a while.
A mind challenged,
Will assumptions defile
Sweet bromides are
For feeble minds,
Trite ideas,
Evil notions find.

32. UNWINDING

Do the shadows of ideas,
I pluck out of my brain,
Only take form
In the obscurity of pain?

Is the dim frontier
Of emotional turmoil
Really needed
To unwind the good coil,
To climb down the precipice
To glory, does it really take toil?

33. It's Trayvon's Brother

Trayvon agreed,
Arms crossed, dread-
Locked, his brother
Was indefensible;
Blowing from some serpent
Stereotypes to oxen.

The news
Got the boy's fuse;
Wrecked, obtuse self-
diagnosis, chronic
Anxiety
Of the medical variety.

Jittery with mass
Incarceration,
The good oxen left
To starve,
While the serpent
Has his fangs out, ready
To carve
Trayvon's brother aa.

As good and evil go,
He had on his right,
A strong coalition -
A chance to redeem himself,

Deliverance through
The dragonfly
Denomination, guaranteed
Salvation.

Seekers sought strength,
They had the clarity
To establish mental parity,
Cherry-picked
Change, called to combat,
They could mediate
A new reign.

He now saw,
He had the tools
But the question remained -
Did he, in fact, choose change?

Agents of the
Dragonfly denomination-
Angelou, Stevie,
King, Barack, and Billie.

-Based on Jean Michel Basquiat's *Acque Pericolose*, 1981

34. HANNAH

Ebullience of a regular
Seven-year-old,
Bright brown eyes,
Seeking attention,
A spritely manner,
Maybe in the image
Of her mother,
Like life itself
Sprang forth
From this little fountain
With dancing eyes
Yet, the silliness seemed
To have left her,
When her mother left her
Marital home
There were no apparent
Marks left of what
She endured.

Her motherly
Physique pristine,
Except for the violence
Of furtive glances,
Sudden movements sent
By the sympathetic nervous system,
Her body, at times, in fight;
Other times, in flight,
She woke up in cold sweats,

Spiteful words exchanged
Over the acrimonious battle
To subsist as a single mother.

This child now spoke,
With none of the clownish
Intonations characteristic
Of her peers from stable
Families, in its stead
Her sweet voice had a shadow
Of a plaintive sigh, so that
Her statements seemed to take
You by surprise
As you held your breath,
Wondering why these
Matter-of-fact notes
Had become second nature
To her and if that didn't
Belie a brutality in itself.

She flits ahead,
To another flower
As if already moved on,
For she had been
Sitting motionless -
Almost invisible -
In way too many exchanges
Way beyond her years,
So that when she finally
Spoke up it was
As if she had absorbed

Way more than she should have
And so, a shadow of a sigh
Now became a part of her,
The entrails of her trauma
Escaping every time
She breathed out -
A little note.

35. JOY

'It's a lot of work,' I said,
'This marriage
Everyday,
Day after day.'

And she said,
'So, I've heard,'
Mirthlessly
Having just dissolved
Her own joyless
Union.

'Unless it's with
The right person,'
Not unlike a job
I thought,
Of hobbies made into
Vocations, so you didn't
Have to work
A day in your life.

I have a hobby
And she now
Has the right person
And maybe
That's all the joy
One family
Can hope to find
In one fief time

36. Familial

'That's crazy,'
The songbird said,
When I told her
Of the sway my mother
Held over me.

She won't admit to the part
She played
With her errant goodwill
 In trying to ensure
My security,
She kept calling
A man she thought
I would be happy with,
Who pursued me,
With all the intention
Of offering a golden cage,
The one his mother
Lived in
Before me
And I didn't see
His father's imprint
On him
Till it was too late.

'Don't choose fear,'
The songbird said.

But her friend
Didn't understand love,
Her values, in the image
Of her mother,
Before her
She valued, what her
Mother showed her,
Was of value.

She chose the
Cage, even paid for
The diamond
Latch on the door.

Maybe it is *his*
Mother's naïveté
That lives on in him,
For he cannot see
The bird slowly dying
Of loneliness
In a home
Where not one
Speaks her language,
Even though
He offers her
Most things Maslow
Would be proud of.

37. Epigenetic

Pitter patter of raindrops
Singing in time with the wind
As it knocks on some windows,
Blatantly selective,
It's lack of equanimity,
Shocking for an element
Yet it does create
Its own symphony.
I accept the music.

Trill, the morning is disturbed.
By the sound of you snoozing
Shrill calls of your daily reminder
You refuse to let go of.
Calls back to routine
You wander in from the
Sweet death of slumber
Still rosy eyed from
Your frontal cortex in limbo
Smiling from the engrams
Some mapped before you
I wonder if you see what you saw

38. It's not me, it's you

When your
Compliments
Ring false,
But your criticism
Strikes a chord,
Is it on me or you?
Maybe it's because
You said I was perfect
At 20, not once but
Repeatedly,
And I believed you -
So now, when I'm older,
And my skin has been
Loved up and dimpled
By the years
And my heart and mind
Wrinkled
From trying to love
Your hard ways,
Calling for perfection
From yourself
And me,
And finding
Really the
Antithesis of it,
My brown
Eyes blur:
I am blind to
Whether
It's on me or you.

39. UGH

The wind howls louder
Tendrils of smoke blow in
Announcing, the neighbor
Being called
To nicotine once again
The clock passively
Smokes the hours
Six to the get-together
This evening
I sigh in resignation
As the wind adjusts
Accommodating instead
To the wood and glass in its path
Audible adjustments
Of diaphragmatic breathing

1 2 3 4 breathe in
12345678 breathe out

The wind whistles loudly
As if empathizing
Outraged
Neighborly
Wind chime
Exclaims in-time

And you turn over
Oblivious to it all
A small murmur
Of a nod to this
Hour of shared space

40. Selene

I see my flaws,
But I wish you
Wouldn't point
At them, and
Bring them into
Glaring view,
Your garb
Of honesty,
Does not
Occlude
The ugly
Whether
In you, or me,
It remains
To be seen.

Because I wish
It wasn't you
Who saw marks
On my thigh
As I rose,
Dripping from
The pool at
My sister's house,
At 28, my young
Skin, golden,
Glittering in
The sun, joyous

To have seen
My sister and the smiling
Newborn she delivered,
Six months prior.

Ceaselessly entertained
By my own
Genetics,
I thought they were
Goosebumps,
Not the frigid
Breeze of your gaze
Raking over
My young limbs,
I'm now immune,
But choke
At your gall
When you miss
The glow of the moon
For a few pockmarks.

41. Apollo and Artemis

I love how the sun
Keeps rising
In my eyes, every time
I see him,
Even as he
Casts a shadow
Each time he
Sees me,
As if the light
Is too much
For his blue eyes,
So, he draws the blinds,
Wears them as a cape,
Walks everywhere in them,
Preferring instead
The comfort of night
Than letting the light
Of the joy emanate
From my yellow
Gaze, dilate his pupils,
Not realizing
It's my light he reflects
In his soft glow.

Maybe its
Just as well.
Maybe I'll
Never learn.

The pair of us -
Like our planet -
Can do without
An eclipse.

42. The Sun

Like a dew drop
At dawn,
At first light
He is born.

Rising every day
In ceaseless strife,
A Shakespearean travesty,
A rebel in his own right.

Maybe he fought
In longing for a longer drought,
Either way I saw him rise
At first light.

So, when he thought:
"Our love might end"
The sun
went right on shining.

- Based on Joan Mitchell. *Daylight*, c1975.

43. PTSD

And just like that,
When I thought
I had healed,
My battle scars
Seem to un-scab
And bleed
Spontaneously
At the memories
Of the callously
Cruel words
Thrown about me
With little care,
So, I just stare,
Making my disbelief known.

I fight, at times
Choke up,
Just vigorously
Shake my head
As if trying
To shake off
This unreal
Moment in time,
Not believing
It was happening
Even as I was living it.

44. Oh Captain, my Captain

I may not have
Lived enough
To move you
With words
That build up
In a wave-like
crescendo
Thundering down
In splashes,
Spraying you
With sea mist,
Words calling you
Like white gulls
Against the white sea foam,
Their yellow bulbous beaks
Open in wild cries,
Wingspan
Flapping by your
Unwilling ears,
You wave them off
As you float
With me through
These lines,
Acting as buoys,
Keeping us both afloat,
Sails wafting in the strong
Winds of these words.

But maybe
I do have
Enough lived
Experience to
Trigger knots
In your chest,
You'll need
To unravel -
Counterintuitive
To your
Lessons naval.

45. Cyclops

I don't interrupt you
As you narrate
In a few words
Months past
There is an errant
Twitch, a shrug
And a frown
My ember eyes
Sear into
Those months
Trails of heat
I sense, unbeknownst
To you, giving you
Grace, a shroud
Of violet haze
We play pretend.
I only see
The lighthouse
You point at
And not the
Cracks in the
Colossus
This Cyclops
stretched
Out in the expanse
Of your years
He luxuriates
In his wake

I help you
Onto the raffa
A respite from
Phosphenes
Seared into
Your surprised
cells

46 LONG DISTANCE RELATIONSHIPS

A thought eclipsed,
A shadowed dream,
A fear surfaced to reveal
A scream,
Encrypted astral tendencies
Are brought to the fore,
Whirlpools pull in the occupants,
Lurking at quiet corners
They are hugely rampant.

The sea, it fathers
Heinous beasts,
Inflicting atrocities
And heralding defeats,
Grandiose of corals, of shells, of pearls
Discerned I, sharp rocks, weeds, their twirls.

Its eloquence envelopes,
Silk greets me
As sand disavows my fate,
Wondrous its persuasive stand,
I am now in its sway,
Sinking with a smile,
Scorning the sea,
Sniggering at his guile.
Flouted the law,

I can't flail my arms.

It's Eden all over again;
I gave in to forbidden charms,
Dark and unyielding,
The waters, they run deep,
Tackling the tide,
Marveling through,
What they did seep?
A doubt, it looms,
A cloud overcast -
Thunderclaps, I've heard,
They never last.

On a plank, with an oar,
Away from the shore,
The carefree crave
Gives in to awe
At the ravenous roar.

The wind whistles
Its murmurs in a pitch, soft,
Can rekindle the fire
Or destroy the loft.

Trying to weigh in
For faith strong,
A venture I suspect

To be long.

Unnerved, I turn inward
In my mind's eye,
I'm back on the shore;
A heartening lie.

- Based on *Hero and Leandro (A Painting in Four Parts)
Part I* by Cy Twombly

47. SO, WHO IS IT GOING TO BE TODAY?

Today is brighter
Than it was at 70 degrees
At noon yesterday,
Hope is bubbling again,
Caged in the pleurae
As if the membrane
Can contain
Its joyous effervescence.

Today I can travel to places
I only wondered
About yesterday,
It's the ebb and flow
Of my 34-day cycle,
Every day a mood
Springs to life
Like a Jack in the box,
Except this box
Seems to reveal
A different
Jack every day.

48. A GOLDEN CAGE

He is generous,
Although not kind.

He is there for you,
Usually without
Warmth for your side.

He is funny
At your expense,
Little wonder
Things are tense.

The colors are great,
But what is fall
Without a blanket, warm,
Like going to the beach
On a day with
No sympathetic sun,
Lingering with pets,
When you are
Allergic to their fur,
It's shared domesticity
With contentment, none,
A cup of coffee, Colombian,
That tastes like ash,
Sweatpants that make you
Itch and scratch,
Wreath of lilies

With thorns in their midst,
Tumbleweeds floating down
Halls in a cold draft.

Words in a vacuum,
Dying of a draught,
Taunting, shadows
Dancing out
Of reach of lamps,
Unyielding, unrelenting,
Unforgiving pacts.

49. Who's calling?

These conversations with you,
Are never not potent
Like land mines
Strewn about in Eden,
We attend to your need
To tell me who called
And where they are at in life,
Always with your agenda
Slightly out of view,
Hiding up your sleeve.

I'm almost hoodwinked
Because I never quite see
The tiny pink leaflet
Of items you think,
Are missing
From my life,
Your first born,
Before you take
Your final call,
So, I can have
Someone to call,
To tell them
Who called
And where
The caller
Was at in life.

50. BIGGER, BETTER, STRONGER

Beset again,
Familiar stirrings,
Feeble at these
Not-new failings
To help my parent
While she relays
Stories of her
Many confidants,
Those with success
In business; those
With beautiful homes,
Those fifty minutes
From their kids in LA,
While her first born
Lives an ocean away,
Out of reach of her
Weathered hands,
Living an average,
Everyday migrant life -
Success that she,
Herself, did not see.

These tid-bits
Trigger me to stay
Hungry, set my sights
On what can still be
My savior complex,
Very showy

With a need,
To build bigger
Successes for her,
So, at last,
She can turn inward,
Her eyes not straying
From what is,
And what has
Always been.

51. Golden Child

A story I tell of a golden child;
Blessed with rhythm, sight and locks so wild.
Her spirit rose with the written word;
Draped in ink, nose high, frame assured.
Her truth as only she can tell
Sprung from the pen and on the paper — there it fell.
Truth that takes you closer to joy
Is God itself- there is no ploy.
Joy that makes your eyes light up-
Is word itself- find it, let it run over your cup.
And all this time, she strove to find a vocation, a career- oh
what a crime!
For days when from paper her pen was bereft,
Her heart felt lost, her intuit was adrift.
Starry eyed about stories, she picked songs- for their lyrics.
And when it was time to choose friends- she picked them
for their limericks.
Now although her good heart did steady stay,
She felt the need for it to race away.
She tried editing, auditing, baking, and pottery.
She took up flying lessons- even tried jugglery.
Nothing charmed her- oh what was this sorcery!
So she took a vacation, and travelled a while.
To clear up the cogs- it was all so vile!
She sat on a beach- her head full of sand.
Listened first to the waves,
Then reflected in a manner grave.

Finally, her true nature surfaced, uninhibited- like her locks
wild.
As her thoughts formed silhouettes
Of ideas fresh and new,
She realized that a mind this fertile
Does not come in twos!
(Well, not unless a steady diet of rhythm is imbued!)
She bowed to her inner God,
To help her find the right chord.
For when rhymes took flight from her pen,
Her heart rejoiced times ten.
And that is the story of the golden child.
Blesséd by Israfel,
With rhythm, rhyme and locks so wild.

52. ADHD

A vacuum formed
Between my ears
So that I couldn't
Focus and breathe
At the time, when
Reading a line
From 'how to code'
Over and over again,
As the pressure built up
Behind my eyes
Like I was many
Feet deep
In a vast lake
With the water
Pressing down
With all its height
Till I was distracted
By a spot of dust,
Too untidy for my
Cluttered mind,
Wanting to control
A small aspect
Of physical space
In my life, even
As my mind

Ran helter
Ran skelter

Against my say,
Till I was
Out of time
Or out of breath
Or out of say
And it was
8 hours later
But I was still
On that one page
From that morning,
And certainly
Hadn't learnt
How to code.

53. Purple skies

No man is an island
Yet my storms are
Gentler without trading
Strangled hellos with
Forced acquaintances
Meaning lost like seashells
On my purple beaches
As I hold my breath
Till the skies clear
And the stranger leaves my door
And my breathing normalizes
As I contemplate
The happy desertion
Knots dissipate with
The disappearing
Unnecessary

54. Into-me-see

You can blame it on
Your busy days
Or my rigorous
Schedule,
But the truth is,
Even when we
Are face to face
You never
Truly engage
Like I'm not here,
Like you see
Through me
To your next
Deadline,
Or golf game,
Or that necessary
Email that cannot
And must not wait,
Or the family member
You must attend to
Like looking into my eyes
For an extra second
Will be too long,
Like I may see
Some untold secret
That wasn't for me to see,
Like any intimacy -
Aside from the

Rudimentary crude
Gesture -
Is a privilege you cannot
Afford or refuse
To partake in
Or will not share with me,
Like the clock
Suddenly speeds up
When I'm looking
At you a second longer,
Longing it to slow
Down, take a moment,
The tick tocks
Faster like
It cannot get away
Fast enough.

When you do take
Pause in public,
Maybe secretly
Thanking your stars
To be at a distance
From my probing brown
Eyes, your hazel ones
Darting with a glass
Of wine seem
To pick something
From the routine
Of our daily mundane,
As if to lull my gaze,
Have my dusky

Eyelids droop a little,
So you can go back
To looking through me
To your next deadline
Or golf game,
Or that necessary
Email that cannot
And must not wait.

55. THE DAUGHTER OF ARMENIA

Unaccustomed to artifice,
Her eyes hold my gaze -
Steadfast,
Reminding me of unkept promises,
Failed resolutions
And every procrastination last.

Here I am,
Held accountable,
Locked in their gaze -
Steadfast.

Her expression
As sure as stone,
Self-assured,
Grey tone.

The silence
Of red brick walls,
Unyielding
In gales strong,
Steadfast, she knows
The fiddle fig died
On my watch,
Leaving the Ficus
Weeping.

Weeping, it waited,
Under the cloudless sky
As the sun bore down -
Its shine steadfast.

Each hazel eye
Wearing twilight,
Unblinking midnight blue,
Gave away no clue,
The shadow gave away
The bent;
A slight unsurprised
Tilt of brow.

Severe, slender neck,
It mounts
A forthright crown
Of curls.

No sympathetic
String of pearls
Serve to distract
When the fury unfurls.

Did I think
I might get away
Without
Diligence due?

If only
I had any sway
Or had some
Some trust accrued.

- Based on Ralph Clarkson, *Nouvart Dzeron, A Daughter of Armenia* (1912)

56. THE LINE IS A DOT TO YOU

Boundaries exist for a reason -
But what if your parent
Is never mired
With uncertainty for when
She has breached yours
With a surprise
You do not require,
Although the tussle
That follows
Where you resort
To anger to have
Your boundary
Reinstated
Always follows
With regret
On your part,
Never hers
Because she
Is preaching
How you should
Be more flexible
When you really just
Have 45 minutes
To get dressed
And catch your bus
20 minutes away
From her house
As she resists reason

To agree that
You need to be early
To board with relief.

Leaving nerves
Behind
In this battle
Ground of grouse,
Surrounded by trees
Of mountain ash and
Green tallow berries.

57. Sorority

I've known you
To pass judgement,
Quick and decisive,
Comments incisive
Meant to lacerate
You don't berate,
You can't physically
Whittle me to dust
With your unkind words,
Yet I find myself trussed
On guard,
Flinching, weary
Of your judgement of me,
I've not known you
To show compassion,
You are not kind
Even to yourself,
I guess it's meant
As reassurance
For why would I deserve
Kind words
When my back is turned?

58. CELLMATE

Word to the wise,
as the wise man might say,
But in all my wisdom,
I cannot obey
The little voice
It's been singing the same song
As I try and try
to keep it down,
I reach and I reach
for the volume control,
For really anything I troll:
Tune, lampoon or meditate;
As the years slip past me like eels.
Penn line after line to have it abate,
The same little voice
Till it starts to grate.
I thought, with time,
 I'll numb it down,
My boundaries might blur,
We won't hear a sound
But time hasn't
its magic spiel
As this wasn't a wound
to heal,
This little voice,
it clung to the bars,
It rattled them,
while I wrote memoirs

It called attention to itself
and all I did was let wheels spin

So only respite I can claim now
is that its occupant still regales.

For what would I do with a hollow cage?

59. SLIP

And once more
She was faced with wrath,
Her kindness met with indifference,
Her inquiries with impatience,
Her concern with annoyance.

Out of her hand
She often forgot
This cherished form in clay
Had been through the furnace
And was hardened by the fire
Bisque, now glaze ware.

Her dark eyes kept searching
even though it seemed
Like this familiar
Lissome form that
Came through her
Was a stranger,
Her ways strange,
Her ideas foreign
Yet she sought
Even when all was
Fraught, to
Salve the loneliness
Of her days
For the day
When this form in clay
Would be malleable again.

60. SOLUTIONS

These incessant
Messages -
Meant to bridge
The gap, bring
Me closer to where
You exist in your silo
Of mountain ash
And green tallow berries.

They never have the
Intended effect,
Beleaguered instead,
I set fire
To the bridge,
Fanning the flames
With expletives
To return
To my peaceful
Meandering.

My oasis now
Closed to
Doorbells ringing,
Relentless in their
Attempt to connect
To my silo.

61. DULCIUS EX ASPERIS (SWEETER THROUGH DIFFICULTIES)

Sunday morning
Designated day to clean out
The little knots of the week
Tease out the dust bunnies
Water the parched plants
Empty the surfaces
Of the weekly reminders
A match in the background
Perhaps a cause for celebration
In this ritual upheaval
Maybe I swallowed a
Peach whole with my
Morning Coffee
Consumed whole
With my list.
Now the pit
Turns in my gut
Restless,
Perhaps, for deeper rest
Than my shallow
Entrails provide
It still sprouted
Some despair
As I watched
Wondering which
Sunday to schedule
This repair

62. VAGITUS

Like I don't remember
Being smothered,
My will negated,
Invalidated,
Guilting me into thinking
My lack of say
Was, in fact, love.

This helplessness
I was learning,
Was affection,
Hounding of my space
Was concern.

It's no wonder
My say made
Itself known,
Bursting forth
In aggressive notes,
Their violence
Violating
My otherwise
Quiet visage,
With aversion I could
Not yet place.

It's no wonder
I shy away,

Your pleas
And threats
And guilt trips
Repulse
My lack of say,
Stowed away
Any pure emotion
Except for distaste,
Too complex
For my mate,
He questions
My cargo,
Why indeed
Would I
Lug around
This freight

63. Chicago Deconstructed

Dark crowds swaying to the beat
Of a new drum,
Like the silver
Sliver of white noise,
Aware yet oblivious
Of their own hum,
Rhythmic slaves, they advocate
Propound,
Till at last
The wheel breaks -
There's a hush;
Not one sound.

Dark lives
Unravel, unfold.
Slow dismantle
Of silver silk thread,
Like wild roots
Severed;
Then shaken free,
Of dark lives they did hold.

- Based on *Autumn Rhythm* by Jackson Pollock

64. TRY AGAIN

My dad says
'There is beauty
In trying,'
Yes, I'm trying
But I'm also failing
With an alarming
Regularity,
I throw caution
To the wind,
Send help,
Find my risk tolerance
So, I don't find myself
In these high risk
Conundrums,
Guessing arbitrarily
Everything
Out of left field,
Blind estimates
Out of proportion
From where
The answer
Needs to be
Like I'd have
Infinite turns
To play at life
Like I'd never
Run out
Of wherewithal needed

To play this
High stakes roulette,
Just so in the end
My dad can say
At least, I didn't
Fail to try.

65. SOPHOCLES

Over and
Over again

Reprimanded
For wanting
An escape,
Where two
Solitudes meet
And protect
That shared
Solitude,
You are not whole,
You cannot
Stand guard over
My solitude
With your need
To run to
All and sundry,
To give away
Your solitude
Like you are
Strangers
And she is
Not your
Closest ally.

Not knowing
That every

Chance you get
You betray
Our shared
Solitude.

66. DREAMS

After years
Of just flapping
My nonexistent
Feathered wings,
Learned helplessness
Against gravity -
Weighed down -
Even when lifted
Off the ground,
I couldn't carry
These wings
To an elevation
I could call *'power'*

Finally, today,
My dreams
Allowed me
to soar
Past my peers,
Who soared
Where I could see

I was where I needed to be.

It was easy -
Like living -
Like gravity
Was a work

Of fiction.
Mid-air
All along
I had weighed
Not a thing.

References

Anne Simonson (1998) Pieter Bruegel's *Magpie on the Gallows*,

Simic, Charles. & Cornell, Joseph. 1992, *Dime-store alchemy : the art of Joseph Cornell*

Guest, Barbara. 2002, *Wounded Joy*

Gander, Forrest. *Eye Against Eye*

Barthes, Roland. 1979, *Cy Twombly: Works on Paper*

Berger, John. 1985, *Selected Essays: The White Bird*

Guest, Barbara. & O'Hara, Frank. 1989, *Post Modern American Poetry*

Schuyler, James. & O'Hara, Frank. 1945- 60, *The New American Poetry*

Schuyler, James.1969, *Collected Poems*

Williams, W.C. 1935, *A Chinese Toy*

William, W.C. 1950-62, *Pictures from Brugel*

Auden, W.H. 1940, *MUSEE DES BEAUX ARTS*

Jean Michel Basquiat's *Acque Pericolose* , 1981

Ralph Clarkson, *Nouvart Dzeron, A Daughter of Armenia* (1912)

The Liver is the Cock's Comb, Arshile Gorky

Cy Twombly: *"The Fire"*

Sally Mann- *Deep South, Untitled* (Weyanoke Estate, Louisiana), 1998